Life Of Joseph Livesey: Founder Of The Temperance Movement

Abel Howard And Son

In the interest of creating a more extensive selection of rare historical book reprints, we have chosen to reproduce this title even though it may possibly have occasional imperfections such as missing and blurred pages, missing text, poor pictures, markings, dark backgrounds and other reproduction issues beyond our control. Because this work is culturally important, we have made it available as a part of our commitment to protecting, preserving and promoting the world's literature. Thank you for your understanding.

LIFE
OF THE LATE
JOSEPH LIVESEY.
FOUNDER OF THE TEMPERANCE MOVEMENT.

ABEL HEYWOOD AND SON, 56 AND 58, OLDHAM STREET, MANCHESTER.

ONE PENNY.

LIFE OF JOSEPH LIVESEY.

"THE announcement of the death of Mr. JOSEPH LIVESEY," says a writer in the *Manchester Guardian*, "will be received with sincere regret, not only in his native county of Lancaster, not merely in his fatherland, but wherever men are disposed to render honour to sterling worth, force of character, and honest endeavour for the public good."

Mr. Livesey, like his co-worker in the early temperance reformation, Henry Anderton, was born at the village of Walton-le-Dale, near Preston, on the 5th of March, 1794. His parents died of consumption in the year 1801, leaving their child to the care of his grandfather and uncle. John Livesey had been one of the earliest makers of cotton goods in the district, but when the business he left came into the inexperienced hands of his father and brother it did not prosper. For three or four years they struggled with increasing embarrassments, and did not relinquish the concern until the savings of a lifetime had been lost. The Liveseys sank back into the deepest poverty, earning a scanty subsistence by hand-loom weaving. The early occupation of young Joseph was that of "bobbin-winder," and after the death of his grandmother, that of housekeeper of the damp cellar which served them for "parlour and kitchen and all." As soon as possible he was promoted to the loom, and wrought at it until his 21st year. In addition to what may be called its normal dampness, the cellar was occasionally flooded from the Ribble and the Darwen. It was probably to these unhealthy surroundings of his early years that Mr. Livesey owed the tendency to rheumatism evidenced in the after-part of his life by four attacks of rheumatic fever and by seven years of chronic rheumatism in his lower joints.

The weaver boy had a keen hunger after knowledge, but the means of satisfying it were in those days very scanty. He managed to procure an occasional book, and learned the difficult arts of reading and weaving at the same time. The book was laid on the "breast-beam" with a cord slipped over the leaves to keep them in position. Head, feet, and hands were thus fully employed. In this way he managed to master the mysteries of grammar and arithmetic. Like most of his class he had a strong interest in the controversial aspects of religion, and one of the first books placed on the two slips of wood hung by a cord which constituted his first bookcase were some volumes of Jones's "Theological Repository." For a time he attended the Parish Church, and was one of the ringers, but in 1811 he was admitted as a member of a Baptist church in Preston. The congregation was too poor to pay the salary of a minister, and their internal dissensions caused Livesey to leave them. He now joined the "Scotch Baptists," and was sometimes called upon to "exhort" the assembled brethren. Is was whilst thus engaged in the old Coldhouse Chapel in Manchester that he met Miss Jane Williams, who afterwards became his wife, and who, for a period of more than half a century, was a sympathetic and affectionate helpmeet to him. A bequest of £80, payable at his majority, enabled him to furnish a small cottage, with a garden attached, and on the 30th of May, 1815, he was married at Liverpool. Next morning their honeymoon tour was made from Liverpool to Walton-le-Dale, where they settled down to their daily toil. They soon found reason to remove to Preston, but the prospect so far from brightening became one of increasing gloom, as the country began to feel the effect of the Corn Laws. Food was dear, labour was scarce, and Livesey found himself, with a delicate wife and an increasing family, in a state of health so indifferent as to need medical advice. The doctor gave the cheap advice so often tendered to the poor, that he should live better, and in particular advised some cheese and malt liquor to be taken about 11 in the forenoon. They bought a bit of common cheese, paying for it at the rate of 7d. or 8d. per lb. It was the time of the Lancaster Cheese Fair, and Livesey heard someone say that prices had declined to about 50s. per cwt., or about 5d. per lb. The thought occurred to him that if he could purchase a whole cheese and retail it to his neighbours, it would be a benefit to all. He found a farmer willing to sell at an even lower rate, and managed to borrow from a friendly draper a sovereign with which to buy two cheeses. After selling to such of the neighbours as cared to buy he stood during the remainder of the Saturday afternoon at the bottom of the Vauxhall Road, and at the close of the day found that the profit—1s. 6d.—was far more than he could possibly have made in the same time by weaving. Chance had thus opened out an avenue to competence if not to fortune, and although he did not immediately cease to be a weaver, the cheese trade managed by himself and his equally industrious wife soon increased to a degree that demanded all his energy and attention, and gradually developed into one of the largest businesses in the North of England. In 1827 Mr. Livesey was foolishly induced to become a sleeping partner in a cotton business, and was left by the principal to settle with the creditors. He paid them all in full, but in doing so sacrificed all his savings, amounting to about £1,600. However, he began afresh his career of economy, and profited by his bitter experience. In settling an account connected with this matter Mr. Livesey took a glass of whisky with his creditor, and the unaccustomed liquid had the effect of making him feel so unwell that he determined never to drink any intoxicant again. To this step he was largely impelled by the desire of setting an example to his own sons and to those around him in the town who were suffering through drunkenness.

Mr. Livesey having had practical experience of the hardships of poverty, always retained a keen sympathy for the poor, and in many ways sought to help them. In 1824 he wrote "A friendly Address to the Poorer classes," in which he spoke against smoking, " dealing with tallymen," pawning, &c. This was followed by a tract on the " Besetting Sin," in which the evils of drunkenness were set forth, and great moderation was urged in the use of alcoholic liquors. His views on this subject, as we have seen, changed, and his restless energy gives him a claim to be considered the father of the " temperance " movement in this country. There have of course been many remarkable instances of individuals abstaining from the use of intoxicants, and a list of these earlier teetotalers would include the names of many men distinguishd for their intellectual power and for their influence upon mankind, but the organised movement against drunkenness is the creation of the present century. The early history of the movement is exceedingly obscure, and it is difficult to speak with entire accuracy as to its origin. Between 1820 and 1830 there arose in the United States, and in various parts of Great Britain, associations known as temperance societies, whose members abjured the use of spirits and promised moderation in the use of malt liquors. In these associa tions the rich temperance man had no embargo placed upon his wine, nor was the poor man "robbed of his beer." Mr. Joseph Livesey threw himself into the work with characteristic ardour at the beginning of 1831. "Shocked with the effects of intemperance" and fully "convinced of the evil effects of moderate drinking," he ceased to touch either ale, wine, or ardent spirits. On New Year's Day, 1832, a Temperance Society was formed amongst the young men who attended the Sunday school which Mr. Livesey had founded for their benefit, and in which writing was taught as well as reading and morals. The pledge against spirits was, however, somewhat inappropriate in a community in which drunkenness was chiefly caused by the use of fermented liquors; and in August of the same year the total abstinence pledge was drawn up by Livesey, and signed by himself and John King, who still survives. This was used as an alternative, but by the time of the annual meeting of 1836 the battle of the pledges was over in Preston, and the "moderation" pledge was abandoned amidst great enthusiasm, the bells of the parish church ringing a merry peal in honour of the thorough-going teetotallers. The word "teetotal" was given by a well-known character of the period, "Dicky" Turner, the stammerer, who, either using an old provincial word or coining a new one, observed that "nothing but te-te-total would do." Mr. Livesey cried out "that shall be th' name," and henceforth the abstainers usually called themselves teetotallers in contradistinction both to drunkards and moderate drinkers. Turner was an effective speaker, in spite of the blunders he sometimes made. The most startling of these was perhaps that mixed metaphor in which he declared, "We will go with our axes on our shoulders and plough up the great deep, and then the ship of temperance shall sail gallantly over the land." The Preston teetotallers were animated by the missionary spirit in an intense degree. Thus in 1833 seven of them made a tour during the race-week to the principal towns in the county. They drove in a car with a temperance flag flying, and as they reached each place they sent round the bellman, who announced the time and place of meeting. At Stockport they beat up their audience with a drum! These tours were frequently repeated. It was whilst lecturing in the Oak-street Chapel that Mr. Livesey first saw "John Cassell, the Manchester Carpenter," who for a time travelled as a temperance missionary, carrying with him a watchman's rattle, and afterwards became the founder of the extensive publishing business still bearing his name. In 1834 Mr. Livesey went to Birmingham and London in the interests of teetotalism. Whilst in London, he was examined before the Select Committee on Intemperance, which was presided over by Mr. James Silk Buckingham. His evidence showed that a familiar acquaintance with the poor of Lancashire, arising especially from his habit of visiting their homes on Sunday mornings, had brought him to the conclusion that drunkenness was increasing, and that chiefly amongst the more highly-paid artizans. His suggestions were to increase the price of the licences, and to appoint inspectors to see that the law was duly observed.

One of his lectures on the "Great Delusion as to the Properties of Malt Liquor" embodied the sentiments of addresses delivered in London, Preston, Manchester, Birmingham, Liverpool, Leeds, and other populous places, and when printed had an enormous circulation. It was frequently reprinted, and it has been estimated that over 100,000 copies were sold. This lecture was accompanied by some experiments intended to show the chemical character of alcohol. At Burnley a man who saw the spirit blazing on the plate ruefully exclaimed; "I have drunk as much of that as would have lit all the lamps in Manchester." In 1831 he began the *Moral Reformer*, which, three years later, was succeeded by the *Temperance Advocate*—a publication which in 1847 was handed over to the British Temperance League, and is still continued. In 1832 he opened a small printing office, and for some years a great part of the temperance literature was supplied by him. Many of these publications were also either written or edited by him. In 1844 he started the *Preston Guardian*, which soon attained a good position. In the conduct of this newspaper he was assisted by four of his sons, the eldest of whom acted as editor. This newspaper continued in the family until 1859, when it was sold to Mr. George Toulmin, who had been one of the pupils in the Youths' Sunday School previously mentioned. The sale of the paper included that of the plant, but if Mr. Livesey had not since that date the command of a press of his own, he did not cease to make use of that instrument for the promulgation of his views

Mr. Livesey in the course of his long life saw many changes in Preston. As a boy he witnessed the Guild of 1802, and took part in the procession of the Preston Temperance Society in 1882, where he rode in a cab, and was received by the thousands of spectators who thronged the streets with quiet demonstrations of respect which amounted to reverence. He thus saw five guilds. He was in his prime when the Radical Orator, Henry Hunt, defeated the heir to the earldom of Derby in the parliamentary election of 1830. The old Earl in great anger gave up his Preston house and ceased his patronage of the races, bull-baitings, and cock-fightings, which had previously marked his annual visits to the town, and many thought that Proud Preston would sink into insignificance when deprived of his favour. Mr. Livesey took an active part in this election, and was a persistent advocate of the Reform Bill. At none of these elections was he more busy than in that of 1841, when "sour-pie" was presented as a practical argument of the evil of the sugar duties, which were defended by the Conservative candidates. Protection had a bitter opponent in Joseph Livesey. Ten years before the formation of the Anti Corn-Law League he wrote: "The curse of the country is the Corn Law." He not only spoke and lectured in favour of Free Trade, but for four years and a half published the *Struggle*, which began in 1842 ended in the week the Repeal Bill was signed. Each number had a cartoon, which, although having small artistic claims, appealed in a very direct and powerful fashion to those into whose hands it fell. As the circulation was at one time 15,000 weekly, and many were sent into the rural districts, it may well be credited with a considerable influence upon public opinion. Mr. Livesey and his wife had a stall at the great Free-trade Bazaar in Covent Garden, and he was one of the deputation that then waited upon Sir Robert Peel. He also took an active interest in the buying of freeholds for voting qualifications. He thus obtained votes in five counties or divisions of counties.

Mr. Livesey had a strong sentiment of local patriotism, which was shown in his numerous efforts to benefit the poor of Preston. These would take too long to enumerate, but we must not pass in silence his share in helping to alleviate the sufferings of the operatives when Lancashire was under her dark cloud. Early in 1862 he saw the need of relief in Preston, and at his suggestion a town's meeting was convened for the purpose of opening a public subscription. Mr. T. B. Addison strongly opposed this proposal on the ground that the Board of Guardians should be left to deal with the matter. There was a moment of indecision, and the influence of the learned Recorder might possibly have won, but for the earnest speech in which Mr. Livesey pleaded for a more generous consideration of the case of the deserving poor, who suddenly found themselves cut off from the possibility of earning a decent livelihood. It would not detract from Mr. Livesey's pleasure that the opponent whom he thus defeated was one with whom he had previously had many battles as to the administration of the Poor Laws, Mr. Addison being a champion, and Mr. Livesey a hearty detester, of the new Poor Law of 1834. The subsequent course of the Cotton Famine showed that the Preston relief fund had not been started one moment too soon. It distributed £131,000, and was managed in a manner that secured admiration. Mr. Livesey devoted the greater part of his leisure to this work. Increasing years latterly prevented him from taking an active part in public matters, but he still issued from his pleasant retirment at Bank Parade, overlooking the Ribble Valley, "New Year Addresses," and other exhortations to sobriety, and continued to the last to exhibit the warmest interest in the cause with whose origin he was so closely identified. In person, he was somewhat below the middle height, with an ample forehead and a face that, whilst indicative of firmness, was very far removed from an ascetic type. The story of his life reads like a chapter from "Self-help," with this important difference, that he sought to help others as well as himself. He never forgot his early days, and to the last his sympathies were with the poor, whose privations he knew by bitter experience, whose kindly virtues he recognised, and whose besetting sin he made it the mission of his life to war against.

After an illness which had extended over eighteen days, Mr. Joseph Livesey, the Father of Teetotalism, died at a quarter to three in the afternoon of September 2nd, 1884, at his residence, Bank-parade, Preston. The *Preston Guardian* says that Mr. Livesey had, considering his advanced age, enjoyed excellent health, and only a very short time ago he was driven to Walton-le-Dale to see his former residence and the old weaving cellar in which he had spent his earlier days. On Friday, the 15th of August, he was attacked by a painful malady which had been anticipated and feared by his immediate relatives. He at once took to his bed, and Dr. Hammond and Dr. Dixon were summoned. Those gentlemen have continued their attendance unremittingly till the last. It was seen from the first that the attack was a dangerous one, and the pain accompanying it was at times intense. The veteran, however, bore his affliction bravely, and with great patience and fortitude. His excellent constitution was manifested time after time, and Mr. Livesey surprised his doctors by frequently rallying after the most painful attacks. As the illness progressed, however, his strength failed, and on Monday evening he sank into a comatose state, in which he remained to the hour of his death. On Tuesday afternoon, at the time stated, the patient passed away tranquilly and peacefully, without even a sigh. From the time that Mr. Livesey's dangerous illness was first publicly announced there have been continual personal enquiries as to his condition from leading gentry of the town and neighbourhood, from his old teetotal colleagues in Preston, and from Temperance workers in all parts of the Kingdom On the advice of the medical attendants, however, none beyond his immediate relatives were permitted to see him, and every precaution was adopted to keep him as quiet and free from excitement as possible.

The extent of Mr. Livesey's labours was fully recognized at the Temperance Jubilee, held in September, 1882. The *Manchester, Guardian* on that occasion observed that in every age there have been individuals who with or without "pledge" have abstained from intoxicants. There were, it is said, in ancient Egypt persons who were bound by oath not to drink of wine; whilst amongst the Jews there were the Nazarites, Rechabites, and Essenes, sects and communities who were vowed to abstinence. One of the five commandments of the Buddhists is directed against drunkenness, and Mahomet, as is well known, forbade wine to all the true believers— a prohibition which the Wahabees hold to be applicable also to tobacco, for the smoking of which they have invented the phrase of "drinking the shameful."

No doubt the teetotal antiquary, whenever he arises, will be able to compile a long list of illustrious abstainers, including saints and martyrs, as well as prelates and soldiers. Amongst them, along with Archbishop Baldwin, Johnson, and eccentries like Roger Crab, he would have to mention that Andrew Tiraqueau, who was the author of twenty books and the father of twenty children, and of whom it was written :—

> Here lies a man, who, drinking only water,
> Wrote twenty books, with each had son or daughter;
> Had he but used the juice of generous vats,
> The world would scarce have held his books and brats.

Towards the end of the last and the early part of the presen century, the intemperate habits of the people appear to have led to organised efforts to mitigate the evil. The first American Temperance Society is said to have been begun in Connecticut in 1789. Gradually the news of this movement reached the old country, but it does not appear that any organised effort was made until 1829, when a congregational minister of New Ross, Wexford, Ireland, conceived the idea of transplanting the Temperance Society on Irish soil. The progress made at first was not very remarkable, but after a time associations of this kind arose in various parts of Ireland,

Scotland, and England. By the middle of 1831 some thirty societies were in existence in England, and 100,000 tracts had been put into circulation. The members were pledged to "moderation" in the use of intoxicants, or at most to abstinence from spirits. The reformers' zeal did not extend to malt liquors, which were still considered innocuous. This was not, however, sufficient for the more ardent and enthusiastic. They began to see the difficulty of defining a hard-and-fast line of moderation. Indeed, as early as 1817 an abstinence society had been formed in Skibbereen, in the county of Cork, and two years later there was at Greenock a Radical Association whose members had likewise pledged themselves to use no intoxicants. But it seems as though they intended this rather as a protest against the high taxation then levied on many articles. There was also the Bible Christian Church in Salford, whose membership was confined to vegetarians and teetotallers.

The modern teetotallers, however, date their origin from the 1st September, 1832, when, as the result of much discussion in the existing temperance societies, Mr. Joseph Livesey and six others signed a pledge "to abstain from all liquors of an intoxicating quality, whether ale, porter, wine, or ardent spirits, except as medicine." Of the "seven men of Preston," as they have often been called, two broke their pledge, and of the others one still remains in a green old age. This last survivor is John King who is about a year younger than Joseph Livesey. The early teetotallers were animated by a very earnest missionary spirit, and preached their new doctrine with great persistence and with varying success. They travelled far and near in order to propagate their views, and many amusing stories are told of the way in which they were obliged to enlist the interest of their auditors, and of the devices they found it necessary to employ in order to secure audiences at all. It was during the Preston race week of 1833 that Livesey, Teare, Anderton, Swindlehurst, Howarth, and Stead started out on the first missionary tour ever undertaken in the interests of teetotalism. They hired a trap, and took with them over 9,000 tracts and a small silk flag bearing a temperance motto. In this fashion they visited Blackburn, Haslingden, Bury, Heywood, Ashton, Oldham, Rochdale, Stockport, Manchester, and Bolton, besides halting at several other important villages on the way. Whilst one waved the flag about, another, the fortunate possessor of a good voice, obtained the use of the bell from the village bellman, and announced in stentorian tones the time and place at which the meeting would be held. It was one of the reformed drunkards of Preston who first applied the word teetotal to express total abstinence from intoxicants. "Dicky" Turner has been said to be the coiner of the word, but, on the other hand, we are assured that it was a Lancashire provincialism which he merely employed as many had done before him. The term happened to suit the desire of the early advocates for something marking with precision and distinctness their position in relation to what were now called the "moderation" societies, and hence, for good or for evil, the word was adopted by Mr. Livesey and his associates. The older societies looked with disfavour, and perhaps with something of dismay on the proceedings of these more ardent advocates. But it was in vain that they attempted to maintain their ground, and after various efforts at accommodation an entire separation resulted, and the British and Foreign Temperance Society eventually, in spite of much noble and clerical patronage, died a lingering death. Whether the disruption was due to faults of temper, or if they existed, to which side they belonged, we cannot say, but in any case, after a considerable amount of internal dissension, the teetotallers were left in possession of the field, and it must be said that in spite o the arduous undertaking they had before them they entered upon their work with undaunted energies, and full confidence in their power to convert the world. Their earlier converts were mainly obtained from the working classes, and if the language of the advocates sometimes lacked that "repose which marks the caste of Vere de Vere" they made up for any absence of polish by the earnestness and sincerity with which they prosecuted their labours. Although their missionary efforts were chiefly directed to the working classes, to which they themselves mainly belonged, they were gradually joined by others of higher standing, amongst whom we may name Dr. Grindrod, Dr. Lees, and the present Sir Edward Baines. John Cassell, the founder of the publishing house, frequently made his appearance upon temperance platforms, where he was well known as the "Manchester Carpenter," having signed the pledge at the Oak-street Society. "I remember quite well," says Mr. Livesey, "his standing on the right, just below or on the steps of the platform, in his working attire, with his fustian jacket and white apron on." In 1834 a conference of delegates was held of the various societies in Lancashire, Cheshire, &c., and a second gathering in the following year at the Oak-street Chapel was presided over by Joseph Barker, then a popular Methodist minister, but afterwards widely known as a Chartist. At this meeting the British Temperance Association was formed, and, after various modifications, is still in existence as the British Temperance League. The object was to extend the operations of existing societies and to promote the formation of new ones by the employment of agents and the provision of temperance literature. One of its earliest agents was Mr. Thomas Whittaker, a Blackburn cotton operative, but since Mayor of Scarborough, and who retains all his early fire and interest in the temperance movement. He has still the rick which he used in those early days to summon his village hearers. The presidents of the next succeeding Conferences were Dr. Grindrod, R. G. White, and Lawrence Heyworth. Mr. John Bright was elected a vice-president in 1841, and in the succeeding year occupied the presidential chair. It will be known to some of the admirers of the great Lancashire orator that certain of his earlier efforts were made on behalf of the teetotal cause.

Meanwhile, as the result of much industrious effort, teetotalism was gradually spreading from the north, southwards; and in Wales, the Isle of Man, Scotland, and Ireland, where the labours of Father Mathew produced an immense, if only temporary, effect. The movement at home was also from time to time influenced by the intelligence of what was being done in America and in the colonies. In the United States there arose the Washingtonian movement and similar "revivals," which led to the formation of the Sons of Temperance, the Good Templars, and other teetotal organisations. Great use was made of the press, and some of the most scholarly contributions to teetotal literature came from the other side of the Atlantic. One frequent cause of intemperance amongst the working classes was the fact that friendly societies and similar associations held their meetings in public-houses. To avoid these dangers friendly societies such as the Rechabites arose. The need for social intercourse and amusement created a demand for coffee-houses and other temperance hotels. In most large towns also temperance halls were built as places where teetotalism could be regularly advocated. It would be interesting, if it were possible, to estimate the amount which has thus been spent by the working classes. In Manchester there are now held every week about 50 temperance meetings, where addresses are delivered to audiences amounting in the aggregate to about 8,000 persons.

It was early seen that the most hopeful field for missionary effort was amongst the young, and this has led to the establishment of bands of hope, juvenile temperance societies, children's homes, &c. It is believed that the first children's society of this kind was that organised by Dr. Grindrod, in the schoolroom of the Manchester Mechanics' Institute, in Cooper-street.

The year 1853 witnessed the formation of the United Kingdom Alliance, the object of which is declared in its title to be the "total and immediate suppression of the liquor traffic." It has been said, and we believe with some accuracy, that the idea of this association was in part derived from an article written by the late Charles Buxton, a member of the well-known firm of brewers. Doubtless the passing of the Maine Law raised the hopes of English temperance reformers as to the possibility of legislation. The Alliance, although in one sense a temperance society and a very powerful one, is not so in the sense of its members being necessarily teetotallers. Its first president was Sir Walter Trevelyan, a man equally remarkable for his mental capability and for his philanthropic spirit, and he was succeeded by Sir Wilfred Lawson, whose "gay wisdom" has passed into a proverb. The possibility of communities existing on a prohibitory basis is pretty well demonstrated by the experience of Saltaire and Bessbrook.

In the beginning the teetotallers were regarded with something like suspicion, if not with dislike, by the churches, and it was not until 1862, and mainly, we believe, by the instrumentality of Archdeacon Sandford, that the Church of England Temperance Society sprang into existence. The success which has so far attended ts efforts is likely to lead to the formation of similar associations in connection with other religious bodies where they do not already exist.

The Sunday Closing Act came into operation in Scotland in 1854, and quite recently we have seen similar provisions applied to Ireland and Wales, and advocated for Cornwall. Mr. Winskill, from whose "History of the Temperance Reformation" we have derived much information, calculates that nearly £20,000,000 sterling is spent yearly in this country in intoxicating drinks on Sunday. It would be a long story to detail the successive attempts that have been made to deal with the licensing system in England, or the extent to which in later times these experiments have been influenced by the public opinion created and fostered by the temperance societies.

Great importance was attached by the early teetotallers to the medical aspect of the movement, and they may fairly boast that the progress of investigation during the last fifty years has brought medical science more and more to the side of abstinece. When Joseph Livesey began his labours there were but few of the medical profession who were prepared to take up his extreme position, although several declarations against ardent spirits were signed by medical practitioners in various districts. At Manchester in 1833 seventeen medical men joined in a declaration against intoxicating liquors as unnecessary and pernicious. The first general medical declaration concerning alcoholic liquors was drawn up in 1839, and the second in 1847 was signed by more than 2,000 of the best known men in the profession. The third, prepared in 1871, recorded the belief that the inconsiderate prescription of large quantities of alcoholic liquors by medical men had given rise to intemperance, and urged care in its use. There is now in London a temperance hospital, where the experiment is being made of the treatment of disease without the use of alcohol as a medicine.

The teetotallers have always made free use of the press. This was a characteristic common to them in Ireland, England, and America. Mr. Livesey, who began the *Moral Reformer* in 1831, has been most persistent in his use of the press, and hundreds of thousands of tracts from his pen have been put into circulation. Amongst the notable names in temperance literature are those of the Rev. John Edgar, E. C. Delvan, John Dunlop, James Silk Buckingham, R. B. Grindrod, Benjamin Parsons, Peter Bourne, Dr. F. R. Lees, Mrs. Balfour, Mrs. Ellis, Mrs. Henry Wood, T. S. Arthur, Professor Kirk, Dr. Monroe, Dr. B. W. Richardson, Dr. Thomas Guthrie, and the Rev. William Caine. The economic aspects of temperance have found their ablest exponent in Mr. William Hoyle, of Tottington. There have also been several special liturgies and a host of hymn-books written or compiled for the use of temperance societies, whilst the wonderful pencil of George Cruikshank has given an artistic expression to the sentiment of the movement.

Amongst the latest developments of the temperance reformation should be named the Blue Ribbon movement and the Salvation Army. The temperance crusade began fifty years ago, and has, of course, fallen far short of the desires and perhaps the expectations of its earlier apostles, but it has certainly had a deep and powerful effect upon the social life of the English people.

Such are some of the results that have flowed from the beginning made by Joseph Livesey.

If it be asked what was the secret of his success, the reply is not far to seek. He had strong convictions, an indomitable will, and a firm faith in the strong common sense of his countrymen. He appealed to their reason, with continued shrewd arguments and plain and homely illustrations. He talked in a language that they understood, and every word told instead of flying over their heads into the clouds, as happens with some, who seek to enlighten and guide their countrymen. He knew the wants of the poor from the experiences of his own early life. He knew their strength as well as their weakness, and it was to this strength that he appealed alike in his endeavours, to benefit his native town, to help in the destruction of the Corn Laws, in the creation of a cheap newspaper press, and in the relief of the sufferings caused by cotton famine.

But remarkable as his life was in this respect, his other achievements are small indeed when compared with the mighty importance of the work he began when he signed the pledge of total abstinence from intoxicating liquors, and threw himself with all the strength and earnestness of his nature into the temperance movement. "And assuredly," observes the *Manchester Examiner*, "when the roll of the Lancashire worthies of the present century is complete, not the least honourable name in the list will be the pioneer of teetotalism, Joseph Livesey, the weaver's son, of Walton-le-dale."

ABEL HEYWOOD & SON, 56 & 58, OLDHAM STREET, MANCHESTER.

Printed by Libri Plureos GmbH in Hamburg, Germany